Make your own
jewellery

ANNIKA LARSSON

Make your own
jewellery

PHOTOGRAPHY BY PER TÖRNQVIST/AVBILDEN

BONNIER
BOOKS

There is something special about jewellery...

There is a growing trend nowadays to create one's own jewellery, and the various materials and techniques just seem to be multiplying! Without a doubt, there is something very special in wearing or giving away an item of jewellery that you have made yourself, as you will very soon agree.

Even if you have only a basic knowledge you can still easily create your own pieces to suit any occasion – and while you are making these special pieces, you will also have the double blessing of time to chill out. For jewellery making is, in fact, very relaxing. And the feeling of calm you get is a wonderful luxury in our otherwise hectic lives.

When I began to make my own jewellery, some years ago, the choice of materials was quite limited. But with what's available today, it's possible to find most of what you need literally around the corner.

It's totally up to you whether you wish to follow my instructions as they are, or whether you decide to use another material or technique.

I hope that this book gives you the ideas and the inspiration to make your own beautiful jewellery that will show off your own personality, which after all only you possess!

Good luck,

Annika Larsson.

Contents

Materials 9

Pearls and beads 12

Techniques 14

Storage and tools 16

Single-strand jewellery 18

Single-strand pieces 20

Multiple-strand pieces 22

Multiple-strand bracelet with dividers 24

Jewellery on a grand scale 26

Rings, chains and charms 28

Open-stitch work pieces 30

Crocheted jewellery 32

Twisted wire jewellery 34

Jewellery using nylon thread 36

Swaying pearls on nylon thread 38

Jewellery with stretch appeal! 40

Jewellery using wire and clamps 41

Jewellery that holds its shape! 42

Jewellery of chains and charms 44

Tiaras 46

Jewellery strung on linen 48

Magnetic stones 50

Fabric as an alternative 52

Suede ribbon accessories 54

Rings, ear-rings and brooches 55

Wool and felt 58

Acknowledgements 60

Materials

There is an infinite variety of materials to choose from when you create your own jewellery. I shall try to mention below some of the more user-friendly materials of the kind you may need. Remember that you don't need all of this in order to get started, but it helps to have a choice of what you want and may need.

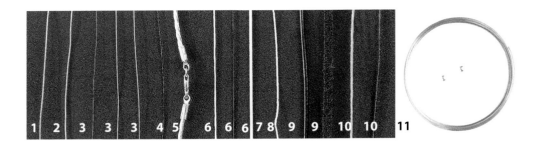

1 2 3 3 3 4 5 6 6 6 7 8 9 9 10 10 11

THREAD

The thread you use forms the real basis of the piece of jewellery, and it depends on what you want to do, as there are so many different sorts of thread available.

1. **Silver wire** can be obtained in both hard and soft forms.

2. **Silver- or gold-plated copper wire** are copper wires of different thicknesses covered in fine layers of silver or gold.

3. **Lacquered copper wire** can be obtained in just a few different thicknesses, for example, 0.4 mm and 0.8 mm. Lacquered copper threads can be found in all the colours of the rainbow. It is easy to work with and can be used for a variety of projects. Just remember that the wire bends rather easily and should probably be avoided in a piece that may be subject to pressure or bumps when finished.

4. **Wire thread** is made up of a number of thin metal strands that are twisted together; the more threads, the more pliable it is. Normal thicknesses are 7, 19 and 49 threads.

5. **Ready-made throat rings** are rigid and simple to use. They can be found in silver and gold.

6. **Elastic thread** is available in various thicknesses and colours, as well as round or flat. The benefit of the flat variety is that it does not slip if you have to knot the work. The knot can also be fixed with a drop of quick-drying glue.

7. **Nylon thread** is excellent to use for pearls. It does not come unwound, and is relatively strong and transparent. Most sewn work uses nylon thread, and also bracelets and necklaces.

8. **Pearl-thread** is made of silk. Silk thread is easy to knot and is used for finer pearl-work, such as fresh-water pearls. It tends to shrink when wet, so should be stretched before using.

9. **Leather thongs and suede bands** are sold by the metre and in different thicknesses and colours. Perfect for threading slightly larger pearls on. Normal sizes are 0.5, 1 and 2 mm.

10.Waxed Linen thread is ideal for long necklaces. Pearls and charms can be knotted on with double knots. This thread is excellent for necklaces and bracelets.

11.Memory Wire is a smart wire that remembers its shape. It can be bought in several different sizes, often labelled for rings, bracelets and necklaces. It is very easy to use this sort of wire and it does not need a clasp to close it. Simply bend over the wire with tongs so that the pearls cannot slip off.

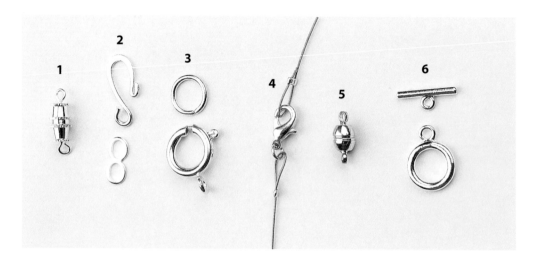

CLASPS

There are a number of different clasps to choose from, depending on the style of the piece you are making and the material chosen to make it in. Here are some of the more common.

1. **Screw-lock** is made up of two threaded parts that can be screwed together. Not always the best for bracelets as they are difficult to unscrew with one hand.

2. **Hook clasp** is simple and made up of a hook which links into a ring. Sometimes it can be two hooks where one fastens into each other.

3. **Bolt ring** is a ring with a spring. The spring is drawn back by a little knob and the lock opens up. The clasp closes when the spring is released.

4. **Carabiner clasp** is a closed hook that opens by pressing a small lever to create the gap for the link to be made.

5. **Magnet clasp** uses two strong magnets. It is opened by pulling the two magnets apart and is closed when they make contact with each other. (Should not be used by anyone with a pacemaker.)

6. **Bar-lock with ring** The bar is longer than the diameter of the ring, and is passed through the ring and then holds fast.

EXTRAS FOR THE JEWELLERY MAKING KIT

1. **Crimp pearls** A crimp-pearl is a little pearl of thin soft metal. It can be clamped together over wire, for example, to set a stop on the thread so that the pearl cannot move. Crimp-pearls can also be used to bind together several threads. Sizes are usually from 1-3 mm.

2. **Headpin/bar** is like a button-needle with either a flat or a small ball head on one end. It is used mainly for making jewels with charms.

3. **Eye-pin.** Has an eye on one end to fasten on to other parts.

4. **Knot-concealer** resembles an open ball with an eye. It is threaded over a knot that is then hidden when the knot-concealer is closed. A lock, for example, is fastened into the eye.

5. **Jump ring.** A link that opens that is sometimes used to join to the clasp, as well as being used as a divider between knot-concealer and clasp. It is also possible to make your own chains of these rings by hooking them to each other.

6. **Ear-hooks.** Can be obtained in several different models and materials. Has an eye that opens to hang charms or pearls from.

7. **Ear-keeper.** The basis of a stud that is worn pushed through the earlobe. It generally has a small eye on which to hang pearls. It can also be completely flat at the bottom so that a pearl can be glued on to it.

8. **Cone.** Can best be used at the start and end of a necklace to hide knots neatly in multiple-thread work. They can be obtained in several forms and materials.

9. **Dividers.** Used to make multiple-thread bracelets and necklaces. They are available as divider-only, as well as with an eye added so that a clasp can be fastened to it.

10. **Different styles of finger-rings in silver or metal.** These can be found, either with a plain plate or with eyes where stones, pearls or charms can be attached.

11. **Brooch-pin.** For attaching pearls and other decorations.

12. **Hair-slide.** For attaching pearls and other decorations.

Pearls and beads

Beads can be found in an incredible variety of materials, from the simplest plastic pearls to designer pieces set with precious stones. Here we've detailed some of the most user-friendly and common beads and described how they can be used. Underneath you can also see some different styles and patterns of threading.

1. **Glass beads.** Glass is one of the most common materials used for making beads. The home of glass bead-making is Switzerland, Italy and Czechoslovakia. Glass pearls are excellent for jewellery and other decorations.
2. **Clay beads** are found in different sizes and forms. They are usually a little larger and work well as a feature on an item of jewellery.
3. **Lamp-work** are handmade beads. They are made by putting pieces of glass of different colours and thickness into a gas-burner to melt. You then make your own beads. It is like painting with melted glass on a glass kernel. The striking beads are often used as the central part in creating jewellery (for example as the eye-catching centrepiece of a creation).
4. **Waxed Glass pearls** are made of glass with a layer of coloured hard wax.
5. **Metallic beads.** Beads can be made of different metals such as gold, silver, brass and tin. These fine Bali beads are made in Indonesia.
6. **Semi-precious stones.** Many semi-precious stones such as agate, rose quartz, smoky quartz, aquamarine, onyx, turquoise, jade, tiger's-eye or hermatite are used in making jewellery. They can be polished into many shapes. These round stones are delicate pink rose quartz.
7. **Stone chips and glass chips** are simple in form and often water-polished so that they do not have sharp edges.
8. **Fresh-water pearls from mussel-shells** can be either from cultivated mussels or wild mussels. They can be found in many colours or shapes. These pearls are very beautiful in jewellery.
9. **Cloisonne** are also called Chinese beads. These beads are shaped first as a copper frame on which copper threads are soldered in a pattern. Then this pattern is filled in with colour and the bead is fired in an oven. Finally it is polished to give it its enamelled surface.

A. **Repeated pattern.** The pearls are threaded in the same way all the time.
B. **Centred pattern.** Start at the middle of the piece and thread outwards on each side. This way you do not start with an eye or a knot, but thread on the pearls first.
C. **Filled-out pattern.** Fill out with smaller pearls between the larger.
D. **Mixed pattern.** Thread the pearls irregularly with no particular pattern.

Techniques

There are many different ways to make jewellery. There are no rules that say you should not mix different techniques within the same piece.

Step 1.

Step 2.

Step 3.

Step 4.

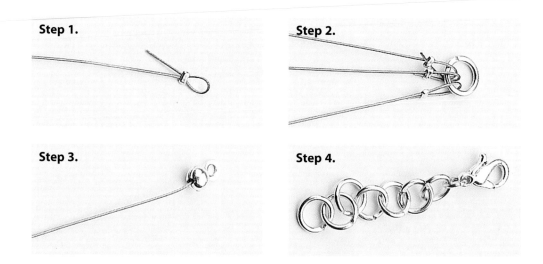

The simplest way to make jewellery is to thread pearls on to elastic thread with the help of a pearl needle. Then make a double knot and fix it with quick-drying glue.

If you use threading that is not elastic, say nylon or wire, you need a clasp so that the bracelet or necklace can be opened. It is different again if the necklace is long enough to slip over the head.

1. **To attach the clasp** is fairly easy and can be done in a number of ways. Without doubt the easiest way is to use crimps. Thread a crimp-pearl on to the thread or wire, make a small loop and push the end of the thread back through the crimp-pearl. Now clamp with pliers. You can now fasten a clasp or ring in the loop.

2. **Multiple-strand bracelets or necklaces** are made in the same way as above. Preferably attach the thread or wire eye directly to the link on the clasp.

3. **Knot-concealers** are best used on nylon-thread when you want to hide the knot. Tie a pair of double-knots and cover with the knot-concealer. Finally, to make it more secure, apply a little quick-drying glue and then clamp the knot-concealer closed with pliers.

4. **Jewellery using rings and eyes.** Simply hook the rings into each other to make the entire piece, or to attach other details to the item. If you plan to use this technique there is a special finger tool that can be used. Two pairs of pliers are also helpful for this technique. Twist the links open slightly, do not bend apart.

CROCHETING IN SILVER AND COPPER WIRE

With a soft and fine silver or copper-coloured wire, you can make open stitching or crocheting either by hand or with a crochet needle.

You can either work with pearls from the start or attach them when you have finished the wirework. If you choose to add the pearls from the beginning, then all the pearls should be threaded onto the wire before you start. Alternatively you thread the pearls onto a similar thread and then tack them on to the finished piece.

The best way to finish off this technique is with a knot-concealer for a single-strand necklace. If you have made a broader bracelet, then metal links, together with a clasp for multiple-strand piece, are preferable.

The thickness of the thread will affect the look of the piece. Thread thickness ranges from 0.18 to 0.5 mm and it is this difference that determines the quality of the end result. The thicker the thread, the harder it is to get an even and fine finish.

A size 2.5 or 3 crochet-hook is fine to start with. If you are experienced at crochet them you may prefer to choose a coarser crochet-hook.

When you are finishing the work, clip off the end and draw it through the last couple of stitches. If you have used a fine strand then you tack the stitches into the piece. If it is a coarser wire you have used, then literally bend the stitches into the item. You can twist the final ends of the wire around the other thread ends in the piece. Then bend the last bit inside the jewellery so that it does not show or scratch you when you wear it.

A simple alternative is to make a long strip of open stitches with the fingers and then tack them together to make, for example, a bracelet.

TWISTING SILVER OR COLOURED COPPER WIRE

Using these wires you can make a frame and then wrap or bind other wires round it. Attach the wire by trimming it off about 4 cm from the bead and stitch the end into the bead so that it holds fast and is hidden. This technique works well for rings, necklaces, bracelets and tiaras. If you want pearls in the piece then thread them on to the wire before you begin to wind it round the frame.

Storage and Tools

STORAGE

Storage is the 'be all and end all' when it comes to keeping pearls, beads and other small articles in order. Boxes with small drawers are fine but tend to take up room. If you have just a few small pieces, such as pearls, beads, tools, clasps, etc, then a file with sealable plastic pockets can work just as well. Such files can often be found in toyshops for those who keep card collections. A file like this takes only a little space and it is easy to see the parts and pearls through the plastic. Another efficient storage method is to keep pearls in small re-sealable plastic bags (usually available at office suppliers).

TOOLS

When you start making jewellery, one pair each of wire-cutting pliers, round-headed pliers and flat plate pliers should be sufficient. It is important that the flat pliers do not have grooves on the inside, or the metal will be marked when clamped by the pliers. If you work using wire or memory-wire, try to have a separate pair of wire-cutting pliers as the wire is very strong and is hard wearing on the pliers. A pair of pliers designed specifically for wire-crimps can be a good idea if you plan to do a lot of work with them. These pliers close the crimps very neatly without flattening them too much, but it is perfectly acceptable to clamp small wire-crimps with a normal pair of flat plate pliers.

1. A **Pearl-needle** is an extremely useful invention because it makes life easier threading pearls with small holes onto both elastic and nylon thread.

2. A **Pearl-mat** is useful piece of equipment. The pearls do not roll around but stay where you lay them.

3. It is very helpful to use **quick-drying glue** to fix knots in nylon or elastic thread. In well-stocked hobby suppliers, you should find a cement glue for use with pearls and jewellery. This cement glue has a very fine nozzle perfect for the precise application of small amounts.

4. A **Measuring tape** is needed for measuring, for both while you work and the finished piece.

5. A **Pearl-dish,** with its three-sided shape, separates the pearls you are using and it is easy to pour them back into the correct drawer or box.

6. Use a **ring-measure** to gauge ring size. A plastic set will be cheaper than one in metal.

7. A **Pearl-table** is useful for designing, and keeping in order, the pearls for a bracelet or a necklace. Arrange the pearls in the order you want them and then thread them afterwards. The big advantage is that you can change and shape a design until you are happy with it, long before you begin to make it up.

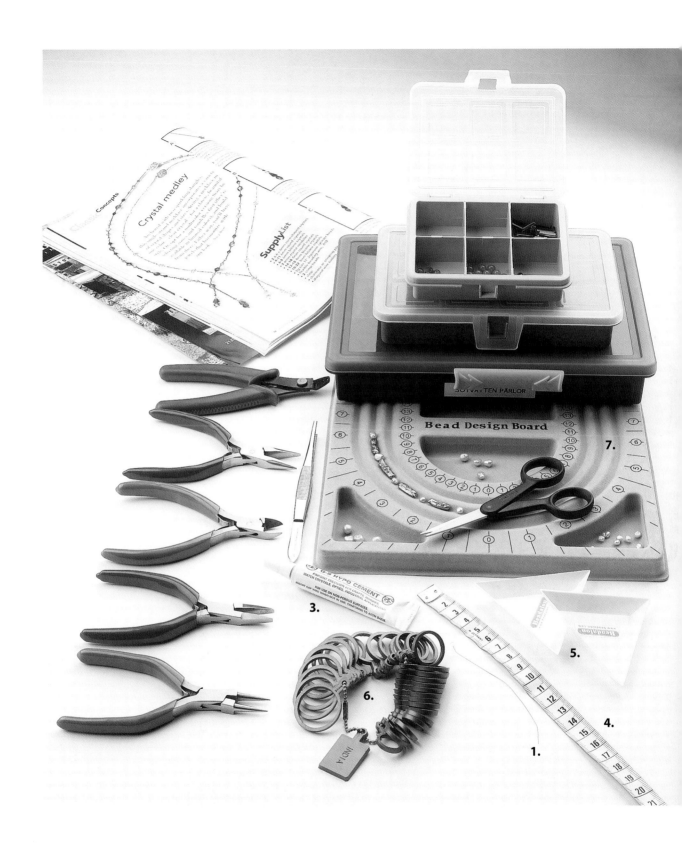

Bead Design Board

7.

3.

5.

6.

4.

1.

Single strand jewellery

Perhaps the simplest jewellery to make is a single strand necklace, bracelet and perhaps ear-rings. First of all select the kind of thread you want to use and whether you will begin and end with wire-crimps, knot-concealers or a knot on a clasp.

This is what you need
- Thread
- Crimps or knot-concealers
- Pearls
- Links
- Clasp
- Wire-cutters
- Plate pliers
- Quick-drying glue (if using nylon thread)

For this I have used wire and wire-crimps, which results in durable jewellery.

1. Decide how long your piece is to be. Add 2 cm for attaching the clasp and a further 1.5 cm if you are making a necklace, and 0.5 cm if you are making a bracelet. These last additions are there because the pearls take away a little of the length of the piece.
2. Thread a crimp, a little way in, on one end of the thread and turn it back to make the loop. (If you do not want a link between the loop and the clasp, then thread the clasp-part onto the wire-loop before you thread the wire back through the crimp and clamp it with the plate pliers.)
3. Close up the crimp with the plate pliers.

4. Now it is time to thread on the pearls. You can thread these on in a variety of different patterns (see page 13).
5. When you are happy with the piece, you finish the work in the same way that you began, with a knot, knot-concealer or crimp.
6. Attach the second clasp part using a link, and glue, as necessary, the knots of nylon thread to ensure they hold securely when you use the item of jewellery.

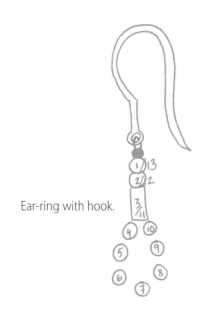

Ear-ring with hook.

Single-strand pieces

Short or long, with charms attached or threaded in a particular pattern – even single-strand pieces of jewellery can be startlingly different by threading in a variety of ways. The possibilities are endless and however you do them, each piece will be unique.

The necklace with a cross is threaded on one piece of silver-coloured wire from one side to the other. I decided on mixed pearls in colours that toned with the cross, and to break it up with some silver metallic dividers.

Halfway through the threading of the piece, thread the wire through the special accessory – an eye-catching pearl or charm – then thread on a further one or two pearls. Turn back with the wire and thread back through the last-but-one pearl and the centre detail and also perhaps through further, already threaded pearls, before you continue to thread on the rest of the pearls on the remainder of the piece. Count or measure both sides so that the necklace is of equal length either side of the centre detail. So what will you have as the centre charm? There is a huge choice available in shops selling material for jewellery making. You may even have something tucked away at home, or can 'borrow' from an old and tired necklace of your own. To finish off, attach the clasp with a couple of links.

Crimps

WIRE

FRESH-WATER PEARLS

BALI SILVER

STONE CROSS

Multiple-strand pieces

Making multiple-strand necklaces and bracelets is as easy as making single-strand pieces – and the results are stunning!

Decide on the number of strands of pearls and the length of the rows. If making a necklace, avoid making the rows all the same length as this will look uneven. Threading the strands in graduating lengths gives the piece a more advanced look. Try mixing pearls of different sizes, colours and shapes. You must use a thread that will be totally reliable if the pearls you work with are a little heavier. Multiple-strand necklaces and bracelets can be made using special dividers. You could also occasionally thread all the wires through larger pearls, equally spaced along the piece, to bring the strands closer together.

The simplest way to do multiple-strand pieces is to start at one end and simply thread through to the other. If you work with wire, use crimps to make the loops in which to attach the clasp parts. You must decide if you are going to attach the wire to the clasp or set a link between the clasp and the piece. For a bracelet you can use a divider that already has a clasp attachment.

To fix rings and lock

Dividers and clasp parts

Multiple-strand bracelet with dividers

To succeed with multiple-strand bracelets, the trick is to take the time to mix and match the colour and shape of beads, to create the perfect item.

It is important to measure exactly so that the space between dividers is the same, regardless if one mixes different-sized pearls. If you use size-matched pearls, simply count to get the same number on every strand, to make the bracelet even.

By using flat elastic thread, dividers and pearls you can create a bracelet without knots or a visible clasp. Also you can get away with not being quite so precise with the length of the bracelet because it is elastic.

You will need:

1. Dividers designed for multiple-strand jewellery
2. Pearls of different sorts
3. Flat elastic thread
4. Quick-drying glue

Multiple-strand dividers

And this is what you do:

1. Start by measuring the length the bracelet needs to be. Add 2 cm for the knot, which you do last of all.
2. Use a thin needle or a pearl-needle so that you can easily thread the pearls. Attach an 'extra-pearl', or paper-clip, to every strand so that the pearls do not roll off.
3. Now thread one of the threads through the pearls you have chosen, before the first divider and then through one of the holes on the divider. Continue to thread through pearls and dividers until you have completed the length (leaving sufficient for the knot).
4. Loosen the pearl or paper-clip you knotted on at the beginning so that you can tie together the two ends of the thread with a double-knot. Fix this with quick-drying glue.
5. Repeat the above process until the number of strands is the same as the total holes in the divider. Your bracelet is ready.
6. It would probably be an idea to glue the double-knots again to ensure that the bracelet is secure.

Jewellery in a grand style

If you are fortunate to have an old piece of jewellery made of beautiful components, try separating them out. Then add to them some newly bought matching pearls to create your own design. You can be sure that no one else will have anything like it!

You will need
- Old or new jewel components
- Matching pearls
- Wire, nylon or strong flat elastic thread
- Crimps
- Flat/ Plate pliers
- Round pliers
- Clasp
- Possibly links

In some craft-shops and catalogues you can find special decorative elements for a reasonable price. It can be a little tricky to finalise the design but that is all part of the fun. Begin by laying out the pearls and considering your design, then thread with the aid of the pearl needle.

If one part is pearls and the other elements are a little heavier, as here, it is better to use a really strong nylon thread or wire, so that it is strong enough.

If you use wire you can fix a simple lock and any possible links, with crimps and the flat pliers.

An elastic thread can also be used here, but if so it should be very hard wearing because the heavy but beautiful components are a weight and the sharp edges can wear the thread. Do not forget to fix the knots with quick-drying glue.

If you have particularly fine elements left over, perhaps you could make a pair of matching ear-rings.

Rings, chains and charms

With links of different sizes, and charms, you can easily make your own jewellery. Using the links or a chain as the base, you can use more links, chains or pearl charms as decoration.

The base can be shaped in many different ways, from a single row with a single charm to a design built up from several chains and charms. If you choose to make your piece from links it is helpful to have two pairs of flat pliers as they make it easier to open and close the links.

You will need
- Two pairs flat/plate pliers
- Round pliers
- Wire-cutters
- Links or chains with opening links
- Headpins or eye-pins
- Pearls

TO MAKE PEARL CHARMS

1. Thread one or two pearls on to a headpin or eye-pin.
2. Use flat or round pliers to shape the pin. Make a bend just a little way from the pearl.
3. Clip off the end of the pin and leave about 1cm above the pearl.
4. Grip the furthest end with the round pliers.
5. Roll the thread round one end of your tool to make a loop.
6. Now you have a loop that can be opened and closed.

You could also do it this way:

1. Thread one or more pearls on a headpin or eye-pin.
2. Use the flat or round pliers to shape the bar. Make a bend just a little way from the pearl.
3. Bend the hatpin or eye-pin about .5 cm from the pearl.
4. Twist the end round the pin to make a loop.
5. Clip off the end as near to the pearl as possible.

Open stitch-work pieces

As a child I learned to do open stitch-work, but in those days I used wool. While experimenting with wire I tried stitch-work using my hands and it worked! I even think this is easier than knitting and it is much quicker.

It is important that the wire used is not too thick, or the fine, even stitches required are difficult to make. The best thickness is 0.2 mm to 0.4 mm. You make a long strip of crochet-work that you then join together to make a broad bundle.

You will need:
• Soft metal thread/wire
• Wire-cutters
• Clasp
• Links
• Pearls

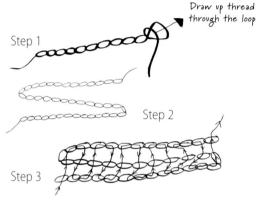

Step 1

Draw up thread through the loop

Step 2

Step 3

This is how to do it:

1. Decide how long the bracelet needs to be to suit your wrist. Do not forget that the clasp is still to be added.

2. Decide how many rows of stitches you want.

3. Make the stitch-work to the desired length. Multiply this length by the number of rows of stitches you want to obtain the total length of stitch-work needed.

4. When you have completed the required number of stitches they must be sewn together to a form a bracelet. This you do by tacking, that is sewing up and down with the same thread you used for the stitches.

5. Fix the ends by winding them round one of the stitches. The clasp is mounted in place using links or by winding it fast with metal thread.

6. If you want pearls on the bracelet they can be threaded on while you do the simple tacking to sew the bracelet together.

Crocheted Jewellery

Some people believe that it is as easy to crochet with wire as it is to crochet with wool. Personally, I think it is a little more difficult, but once you get the hang of it, it is actually easier than you would expect.

If you are already familiar with crocheting, you can start with silver-thread if you wish to. It is more expensive than using silver-coloured copper thread but the result is more durable and more beautiful. If you are not used to crocheting, then practise on a cheaper thread before progressing to silver.

The silver-coloured thread does however have certain advantages, in that it comes in many different beautiful colours. If gold suits you best, you can crochet in gold-coloured copper thread.

It's up to you the direction you crochet in, either vertically or horizontally. Personally, I prefer vertical when I crochet and horizontal when I do open stitch-work. It is just a matter of preference.

The size of crochet-hook you choose is decided by the size of stitches you want and the thickness of the wire you're using. A no. 3 crochet needle is probably about right if you are using wire 0.4-0.5 mm thick.

If you want to have as few wire-ends as possible, try threading the pearls on the wire before you begin to crochet. This is a little more advanced as a technique. But you can also tack the pearls on afterwards, with a similar wire and finish by twisting the ends into the crocheted bracelet.

You will need

- About 25 m silver wire, diameter of 0.4- 0.5mm.
- No 3 crochet hook
- Pearls
- Clasp
- Links
- Wire-cutters
- Round pliers

Do it like this

1. Begin by laying out the crochet-work to the desired length. About 25 open stitches are usually enough for a 17 cm long bracelet if you crochet horizontally.
2. Crochet the stitches forwards and backwards until the bracelet is the desired size.
3. To tidy up and even it out, you can tack overcast-stitches round the four sides of the bracelet.
4. Wind the ends into the crocheted bracelet.
5. Attach the clasp to the two short sides either by winding fast with wire or by fastening with links.

Twisted wire jewellery

It is possible to make fantastic items of jewellery from reels of ordinary florist wire or from inexpensive hobby wire. These reels of wire can come in many different colours. With a little practice you can make some attractive and fine designs.

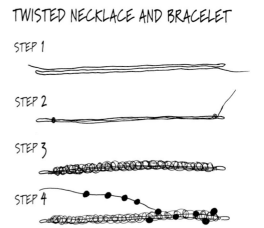

TWISTED NECKLACE AND BRACELET

STEP 1

STEP 2

STEP 3

STEP 4

The idea of these is to twist wire several times around a base of a desired shape. The base is made up of several turns of wire - the heart is made, for example by taking several turns of wire around the hand, before you bend it and shape it into a heart. The ends are bent in by the round pliers and poked in to the piece so that they do not catch or look scruffy. Charms can be hung on chains or leather strings or onto stiff throat-rings. Fix the pearls as the piece takes shape.

There are no rules to follow so see what you can do. The round pliers will be your most important tools. With them you can shape and move the wire to get it precisely where you want it.

If you wish to make a long charm, like that with the white pearls, you must poke it into shape. Special tools for poking can be found in craft-shops. Different poking-tools need slightly different techniques but instructions on how to use them always come with them when purchased.

Wired heart

STEP 1

STEP 2

STEP 3

STEP 4

Jewellery using nylon thread

You can create exciting jewellery using nylon thread and pearls – try making bows, squares and other patterns. Look at the sketches and maybe try out your own ideas and patterns to achieve different effects.

Tips for patterns

Daisy Chain

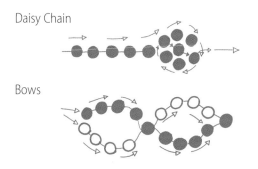

Bows

The advantage of nylon thread is that it is strong and transparent and is found in many different thicknesses. Try looking in fishing sport-shops to find this kind of thread. It is often cheaper there than in craft-shops and what's more, is sold in larger packages.

On the internet you should find many free designs and patterns that show you exactly how to sew or thread this type of jewellery and which pearls to use. If you want to use your own design try sketching before you start. It is important to have a good pearl needle and to keep track of the number of pearls used so that they tally with the pattern.

The knots at the beginning and at the end can be easily hidden by using two knot-concealers.

But remember, every time you join nylon thread you must fix the knot with quick-drying glue.

You will need
- Nylon thread
- Pearl needle
- Knot-concealer
- Clasp
- Quick-drying glue
- Scissors
- Flat pliers

JEWELLERY USING NYLON THREAD

STEP 1

STEP 2

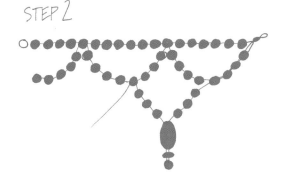

Swaying pearls on nylon thread

'Swaying pearls' refers to the fact that they seem to be floating around the throat or wrist, as the thread cannot be seen. Fine nylon thread with well-spread out pearls forms the basis. Fix the pearls in place with quick-drying glue or with a crimp on either side of every pearl.

You will need:

- Nylon thread, about 0.1 mm
- Pearls
- Quick-drying glue or crimps and flat pliers
- Knot-concealers
- Links
- Clasp

Here's how to do it:

1. Decide how many strands you want and how long your necklace is to be. Add about 4 cm to each row for knots. Measure and cut off.
2. Gather together the threads evenly together and tie in a knot at one end. Glue the knot with quick-drying glue and leave to dry. Clip off the ends on the knot and lay it in an open knot-concealer and close with the flat pliers.
3. Now start to thread the pearls. If you have decided to fix with crimps then you thread in the order crimp, pearl, crimp. Close the crimps properly so that the pearl sits where you want it. If you're fixing the pearls with quick-drying glue, then thread them on one at a time, glue and leave to dry before threading the next one.
4. Regardless of which method you're using, finish threading the first row and leave about 2 cm for the finishing knot that is made when all the threads have been threaded. Continue with the other rows if you are making a multiple-strand necklace or bracelet.
5. When you have threaded all the threads with pearls, gather the ends together and knot together and fix a knot-concealer in the same way as you did at the beginning.
6. Mount the clasp with the aid of links.

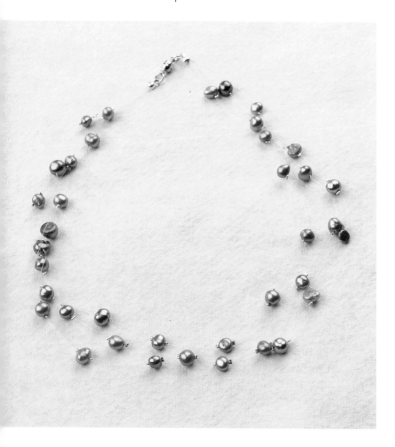

Jewellery with stretch appeal!

Elasticated thread comes in many varieties – different thicknesses, round or flat and in a number of colours, as well as the transparent varieties.

Flat elastic has the advantage that it does not come undone when it is knotted to tie the work together. The flat elastic thread is made up of many fine fibres that have been pressed together so without due care they can fray apart. Elasticated thread can be used for bracelets, necklaces, hair-bands or anything that does not need a clasp.

When you start on an elasticated item of jewellery, fasten one end with a paper-clip so that the pearls do not roll off. A figure-of-eight knot is best for knotting the jewel fast. When you are finished, test and stretch the knots a little to make sure they do not come undone before you clip off the loose ends at the knot.

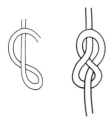

Different patterns to follow

Daisy Chain

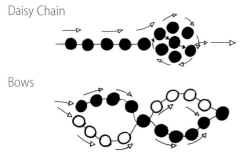

Bows

Jewellery using wire and clamps

With wire and clamps you can design pieces exactly the way you want them to be.

Wire is the most durable thread to use and is, at the same time, attractive to look at. It can be found in different colours and thicknesses. You don't always need to cover the wire with pearls but can allow some to be seen between the different fixed groups of pearls.

You will need:
• Wire
• Crimps
• Pearls
• Links
• Flat pliers
• Wire-cutters

Make it in this way:
1. Decide on the look of your jewel and draw up the design on paper.
2. Measure the wire to the right length and add 4 cm for the beginning and finishing and then cut.
3. Begin to work on the piece from the centre.
4. Work out towards the sides. On either side of one or several pearls, attach a crimp so that the pearls are set in place singly or in groups.
5. Leave a small space between this and the next group of pearls.
6. In each group of pearls, you can also add different length charms.
7. When you have finished threading, matching both sides of the necklace, finish by using the crimp to make a loop in the wire and then set your clasp-parts in place.

Jewellery that holds its shape!

You can make beautiful necklaces, bracelets and rings with memory wire. The beauty of this wire is that it suits everything. You can thread beads in different patterns, hang on charms and finish with luscious dangling pearls.

Memory wire has the capacity to remember its shape and therefore needs no lock. It wraps itself round your wrist or neck and stays in place. Start and finish by shaping a loop of wire with round pliers, or by glueing in place a stop-pearl so that the pearls cannot come off. When you work with memory-wire you should use a separate pair of strong wire-cutters because memory-wire is very strong.

Decide for yourself how many strands/windings you want to have.

For this you need:
• Memory wire for necklace, bracelet or ring
• Strong wire-cutters
• Possible stop-ball/pearl
• Pearls
• Headpins
• Links

And you do it like this:
1. Clip off as many strands/windings of wire you want.
2. Bend a loop or glue on a stop-pearl as an end point.
3. Begin to thread the pearls on as you want them.
4. Thread all the wire strands/windings and finish as you began with a bent loop or a glued stop-pearl.
5. Make charms using pearls and headpins and mount them where you want to have them, for example at the centre of the necklace, or perhaps in the loops at the beginning and end of the piece.

Jewellery of chains and charms

With ready-made links, chains and charms you can make a totally up-to-date piece with short or long, dangling charms. And the more colours, shades and shapes you mix and match, the finer it will be.

Ready-made links and chains are available by the metre in craft-shops. There is also a huge choice of made-up charms to choose from, either in craft-shops at reasonable prices, or more expensively and extravagantly at jewellers' shops and goldsmiths. You could just check your own jewellery collection to see if you have something that might be useful. In craft-shops you can find everything required to make this kind of luscious item of jewellery. If finding the exact charm you want is causing a problem, then you could make your own!

For this kind of piece it is best to work with two pairs of flat pliers. One pair is used to hold the eye that you hang the charm from and the other to open and close the eye. Make sure the eye is firmly closed so that the charm does not fall out.

Finish the work by mounting a bar-lock. It is both practical and pretty in this kind of piece.

You will need
- Link or chain
- Charms
- Pearls
- Headpins
- Links
- Two pairs pliers
- Clasp

Colours that work well together
Red – black – silver
White – creamy-white – beige – old rose
Orange – cerise pink

Tiaras

Are you in the mood for giving an unforgettable gift? You could make a stunning bridal crown. Perhaps you are going to a ball or you simply want your daughter to feel like a princess?

A tiara is a beautiful accessory to have up on the shelf. You'll probably find that the opportunities to use it are greater than you think!

Using the same technique used to make wire-based jewellery you could make a fine and glittering tiara from ordinary coloured or silver wire.

Begin by measuring the head the tiara is intended for. Sketch a design, exactly the way you want the tiara, on paper. Make the basic shape from the wire. If you are going to make a diadem you need to add about 3 cm to each side that you can fasten into and hide in the hair.

When you have made the basic shape simply twist the wire around this until you feel that the shape is firm and it looks attractive. Last of all fasten on the pearls if you wish to have them on the tiara. Hide the wire ends under the pearls and inside the wire work so that the ends are invisible and do not catch in the hair or scratch the wearer.

You will need
• 40 metres of metal wire
• Pearls
• Round pliers
• Flat pliers
• Wire-cutters

Jewellery strung on linen

Using no tools, you can make beautiful necklaces and bracelets of linen-thread, just by knotting your pearls in place!

The beads are spread out on the thread so it is possible to make a long necklace without emptying your store of hard-won pearls! Matching the linen thread to pearls of the same colour, but different shades, makes the whole task even more enjoyable. Linen thread is very hardwearing and no needle is required to thread on the pearls as the strand is waxed and is easily formed into a point. The threading is simple.

It may be a little difficult to find thread in the exact colour you want but it is sold by the metre in some shops.

You can thread pearls onto a long linen cord and avoid tying the ends together. In this way you get a necklace that you wind round the neck several times, wearing it differently every time it is put on! If you do knot the necklace together, then you can hang a couple of large pearls as a charm at the centrepoint.

Or why not tie on a pretty glass cross, or some other large charm, in the middle of the thread. Then thread both linen pieces through some pearls a short way above the cross in order to then separate the threads off in each direction and continue to knot further pearls on each side. An unbelievably simple method - but very effective!

Magnetic stones

You will need

- Magnetic hematite beads
- Extra fine pearls
- Wire, about 90 cm
- Crimps
- Flat pliers
- Wire-cutters

The magnetism in this jewel comes from the black hematite. These beads are magnetically attracted to each other. If you choose to make jewellery of this type it is important that the space between each stone is regular. Then the jewellery will sit tidily and evenly round the throat or wrist. You can thread other different pearls between the magnetic stones. Beads made of Bali silver are especially pretty. Bali silver can be found in craft-shops, where you can also usually find cheaper alternatives not made of real silver.

Do it like this

1. Decide how long you want your item to be. Wire is the best choice for the base of this as it is quite heavy when finished.
2. Thread on a crimp and close it fast at one end and then thread from the other end.
3. Count how many pearls you thread on between every magnetic hematite bead so that have the same distance between each part of the pattern.
4. Make sure that the pearls are not packed too close together, otherwise it will be difficult to wind the jewel round the wrist or throat. Finish with a crimp.
5. The leftover ends should be clipped off with wire-cutter pliers just beyond the final crimp.

Fabric as an alternative

You can make bracelets, charms and brooches from beautiful fabrics and matching pearls. The easiest way to make the fabric framework is by sewing on a machine but you can also sew it by hand. You can sew hearts, stars or round brooches.

You will need
- Fabric
- Pearls
- Transparent or matching thread
- Sewing needle
- Measuring tape
- Scissors
- Sewing machine
- Snap-fasteners or teasel ribbon

This is how you make a bracelet:
1. Decide on the length and width of your bracelet. Add about 2 cm on all four sides as seam allowance.
2. Measure on the fabric and cut out.
3. Use pinking shears to zigzag cut the edges on all four sides.
4. Press the seams on all four sides.
5. Fold the seams to the centre lengthwise, to the width you want it, and press.
6. Decorate the front with pearls and spangles or charms, using transparent or matching thread. Fasten the thread with a double-knot on the reverse side. Space the pearls out a little space making sure the thread between the pearls is hidden on the reverse side.
7. Try not to pull on the thread too much or there will be wrinkles in your bracelet.
8. Sew the bracelet together by turning it wrong side out and then sew in the crease for the seam allowance (in the middle of the reverse side). Turn the bracelet inside out so that the decoration is on the outside.
9. Turn in the edges on the ends and sew a straight seam through the four layers.
10. Sew the snap-fasteners or teasel ribbon on by hand.

Suede ribbon accessories

You can make a very attractive piece of jewellery from the softest suede and there isn't a drop of glue in sight!

Suede ribbon can be bought in craft-shops or from jewellers.

Make six charms of pearls and beads that match the suede ribbon (see page 28 for ideas). Cut a piece of the suede to the desired length.

Thread three charms on a slightly large link, about 0.5 mm in diameter. Close the link and thread it onto the ribbon about 20 cm from the end. Tie a knot in the suede ribbon so that the charm is held fast. Do the same thing on the other side of the suede ribbon. Could it be any easier?

If you want to make something a little extra special you could attach several pearls to each charm.

Rings, ear-rings and brooches

You can make rings in many different ways and with different shapes as a starting point. I think the best are when the rings are a little 'tangled' and uneven.

If you use a ring-frame carry on in this way

Cut a 50 cm length of jewellery wire, eg silver, 0.5 mm in diameter. Twist one end round the ring-frame to hold in place. Thread the pearls you have chosen for the ring onto the wire Begin with the pearls you want at the base of the ring and thread the smallest on last. Place the first threaded pearls over the ring-frame where you want them. Twist the wire a whole turn round the ring-frame and then continue to wind the pearls into place, exactly as you want them.

It is easiest if you use an adjustable ring, as it is then possible to open the whole thing up so that you do not have to thread through the ring.

On the last turn you should pull the wire a little tighter so that everything is set in place.

Finish by sticking the wire end through the tangle and out on the other side and draw tight. Clip it off 0.5 cm from the ring. Twist the end into a spiral with the round pliers and press it into the tangle so that it cannot be seen or felt.

If you want a particular ring size, the easiest way to get this is by winding thread several times round a cork or a bottle of nail polish.

Check and adjust the resulting size. Twist the end several times around the ring-frame and then thread on the pearls and fasten in the same way as described above.

Ear-rings are best made using a headpin or eyepin. Thread with pearls and stones, and then make an eye with the round pliers. Make ear-rings to match your other pieces of jewellery. Long or short is a matter of taste. Just remember that not all ear-hooks are nickel-free, so don't forget to ask when you buy them.

Brooches like this are simply the most stylish I have made and they are so easy too! Try giving a brooch like this as a small gift instead of a flower.

The only things needed for these are wire and wire-cutters. The wire should be pliable enough that you can shape it with your hands. Make the leaves of the flower one by one. Then wind the wire around the leaves, taking the wire up and down between each strand, between every other leaf, wrapping the whole thing together, to make the centre of the flower. The end of the wire that is now on the underside you save as the pin with which to fasten the brooch. The other loose end is clipped off and wound round and into the design.

Wool and felt

You can make beautifully coloured 'beads' that are incredibly soft by using wool or felt. With the help of a felt or blanket-needle you tease up and shape the wool to then make your 'bead'. You can also make decorative pieces of thicker hobby-felt, by clipping out small circles or squares.

You will need

- Felt/blanket/rug-needles for wool-teasing: three different sizes.
- Wool in various colours
- Foam cushion/pad, 5-10 mm thick
- Scissors

FELTING TECHNIQUE

Remember that the needle is very sharp and is also easily broken. Use vertical movements.

You will need enough wool to start with that is just about equivalent to double the volume of the finished 'bead'.

Lay the wool on the foam pad. Begin with the coarsest needle to bundle the fibres in the wool together, the coarser the needle, the thicker the hole in the wool. Take the needle up and down, vertically. Push in and shape the wool at the same time as you stick in.

When the wool is packed together turn the bundle over and continue to tease. By turning the wool bundle over, it is teased from both directions. Change to a finer needle and continue to take the needle up and down. If

you want to decorate the bead with splashes of wool in another colour it is best done with the finest needle that leaves only small holes. Trim off any wool fibres sticking out.

Decorate with pearls or embroider on decorations in matching or contrasting colours.

HOBBY-FELT

You can find felt in different colours and thicknesses in craft-shops. Cut out "beads" in different shapes and sizes. When you add them to a piece you thread with a fine sewing-needle. A beautiful combination is to contrast felt 'beads' with glass beads.

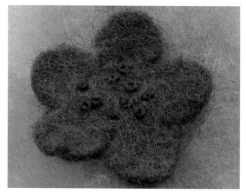

Acknowledgements

Here are a few suggested websites to help you start up.
There are many more!

www.spirit-of-the-past.com
www.the-beadshop.co.uk
www.rockingrabbit.co.uk
www.internationalcraft.com
www.noseksjustgems.com
www.justbeads.co.uk

If you are looking for fine pearls, beads and other accessories

www.artsandcrafts.co.uk
www.beadsales.co.uk

My warm thanks to;

- All who provided pearls and beads for this book, thereby showing all the beautiful colours and shapes that are available out there.
- My photographer Per Törnqvist from Avbilden AB in Borås, Sweden who succeeded so well in transforming my thoughts into pictures. You are the best!
- My small children, Elsa and Erik, who, every day, help me to pearl, to hug and just to be.
- And last, but not least, to my editor Eva Falk and my publisher Annelie Lindqvist of Bokförlaget Semic who really believe in me.

Thank you!

Originally published in Sweden by
Bokförlaget Semic, Sundbyberg
under the title 'Gör Egna Smycken' in 2005

First English language edition published by Bonnier Books 2007

Bonnier Books, Appledram Barns, Birdham Road
Chichester PO20 7EQ

Bonnier Books website
www.bonnierbooks.co.uk
ISBN 978-1-905825-27-1
Printed in China